PEREGRINE FALCONS

First published in Great Britain in 1991 by
Colin Baxter Photography Ltd.,
Unit 2/3, Block 6,
Caldwellside Industrial Estate,
LANARK, ML11 6SR

British Library Cataloguing in Publication Data
Dennis, Roy, 1940 –
    Peregrine falcons.
    I. Title
    598.918

ISBN 0-948661-27-5

Photographs by

Front Cover © Michael Leach (NHPA)
Back Cover © Richard T. Mills (Aquila)
Page 19 © E. Murtomäki (NHPA)
Page 20 © Roy Dennis
Page 21 © Wendy Shattil/Bob Rozinski
Page 22 © B. S. Turner (FLPA)
Page 23 © Dennis Green (Bruce Coleman)
Page 24 © Roy Dennis
Page 25 © W. S. Paton (Bruce Coleman)
Page 26 © Richard T. Mills (Aquila)
Page 27 Top © Roy Dennis
Page 27 Bottom © Roy Dennis
Page 28 © Stephen J. Kraseman (Bruce Coleman)
Page 29 © E. Murtomäki (NHPA)

Page 30 © Geoff Bates
Page 35 © Roger Hosking (FLPA)
Page 36 © C. H. Gomersall (RSPB)
Page 37 © C. H. Gomersall (RSPB)
Page 38 © Wendy Shattil/Bob Rozinski
Page 39 © R. J. C. Blewitt (Ardea)
Page 40 © Roy Dennis
Page 41 © Richard T. Mills (Aquila)
Page 42 © Roger Tidman (NHPA)
Page 43 © Roger Tidman (FLPA)
Page 44 © W. S. Paton (NHPA)
Page 45 © Wendy Shattil/Bob Rozinski (OSF)
Page 46 © Conrad Greaves (Aquila)

Peregrine Falcon Illustration © Darroch Donald

Printed in Great Britain by
Frank Peters (Printers) Ltd., Kendal.

PEREGRINE FALCONS

Roy Dennis

Colin Baxter Photography Ltd., Lanark, Scotland

Peregrine Falcons

Peregrine falcons are special birds. Fast, powerful and majestic, with a glint of wild places in their eye. Superb hunters of the skies, they catch their prey at high speed in spectacular aerial pursuits. To me they seem only at home when on the wing and most of my memories of them involve flight. As a boy, I remember an autumn evening viewing waders at a coastal lagoon on the Solent when out of the reddening sky a peregrine struck. One second, five green sandpipers on migration to Africa were busily picking in the muddy shallows, the next one was dead and the others had flung themselves headlong into the water or were towering skywards in panic. With lethal precision the peregrine had snatched the sandpiper from the surface at over 100 miles per hour without hitting the ground. Those early experiences all involved passage birds in autumn or winter; sometimes I saw them hunting teal over the lagoons or maybe later roosting in a large dead tree like sentinels viewing the grey coastal marshes.

During boyhood visits to the Dorset or Cornish coasts I had watched them stooping at seabirds or perching on high cliffs bedecked with sea pinks. Since then I can recall many memorable days with peregrines. On a beautiful summer's day while walking in the high Cairngorms I saw one of Britain's highest living peregrines striking a ptarmigan over the Ben Macdhui plateau. Another time while studying migration at Cape Wrath in north-west Sutherland I watched the local peregrine streak off out to sea to hound a tired whimbrel arriving from Iceland. One cold winter morning I marvelled at the skill of a pair of adults flushing Fieldfares in the snow on the Black Isle. Much further afield, I can vividly recall a peregrine pulling out of a headlong dive with a swish of air through its feathers as a pigeon dived into trees alongside the dusty main street of Bulgan at the edge of the Gobi desert in Mongolia.

The peregrine falcon's spectacular ability to catch other birds in flight has meant a long association with man, who used the bird for hunting and sport. Falconry has been practised for 4,000 years and this species has always been one of the most highly prized because of its dramatic skill. How falconry began in the ancient civilisations of the East is unknown but the idea was probably picked up through chance observations and a few free meals, just as I benefited one summer in the Cairngorms when a dead ptarmigan dropped near me when the falcon which killed it failed to hold its prey and I took it home for my supper. Thereafter it became a sport and records reveal that in Mongolia the Kublai Khan had 500 falcons and hawks in the 13th century plus an army of 10,000 beaters for his hawking expeditions.

Falconry has been practised in Britain since the 3rd century and this species has been one of the most famous in our country. In fact peregrines were valued extremely highly and were the property of kings and chosen noblemen. For instance, in 1335, King David II of Scotland sent King Edward III of England a single peregrine falcon as a gift, while the Dukes of Atholl gave the Crown a pair of peregrines as payment for their sovereignty of the Isle of Man. The bird was strictly protected in the wild by draconian measures.

By the Middle Ages more people were involved in falconry and it has been practised in much the same way ever since. The birds are trained to perch on the falconer's hand and are usually hooded until ready to fly. The quarry is located and the bird set free. Circling high overhead, the prey is flushed and the peregrine uses its dramatic skill to catch its quarry in full flight. In olden days, peregrines were flown at herons but nowadays the quarry is usually grouse or partridge. Until 30 years ago they were taken from the wild either as nestlings or trapped on passage. Today most are bred in captivity and to be legal each bird is required to be registered with the Department of the Environment and fitted with a special ring soon after hatching.

Peregrines are crow-sized falcons with long pointed wings and slightly tapered tails. The adults are slate grey above with buffy-white underparts barred black, shading to pink on the breast; the head and distinctive moustachial stripe are black. The strong, hooked bill is black-bordered by a yellow cere; the powerful legs and talons are yellow and the eye is dark brown. Juveniles have brown upperparts patterned with buff and the pale underparts are vertically streaked with dark brown. The female or falcon is larger and darker while the male is usually about a third smaller, thus the falconer's name of tiercel, from the French for one-third. The normal flight is powerful and direct, with long glides interspersed with shallow wing-beats while the stoop after prey can reach speeds of nearly 200 miles per hour. Normally silent, the bird has a range of calls from harsh strident 'kek-kek-kek' to quiet chips and chittering calls, especially near the nest.

The species occurs throughout the world and in fact is probably one of the most successful and widespread of birds. Its scientific name *Falco peregrinus* denotes its membership of the genus *Falco* and its wandering or widespread nature. The German name, *Wanderfalke,* and the Swedish name, *Pilgrimsfalk,* both recall the migratory nature of the bird. There are about 24 races worldwide which vary in size and coloration; they nest on every continent except Antarctica. Some are resident while others, especially in high latitudes, are long-distance migrants. Three subspecies breed in Europe; the nominate race, *peregrinus*, occurs in the British Isles and throughout temperate and sub-arctic Europe. The smaller race, *brookei*, lives in the Mediterranean region and a larger bird, *calidus*, migrates to breed in the Arctic regions of Finnmark and Russia. Throughout the world, they feed on many different species of birds. For example, at eyries in the Falkland Islands, I noted the remains of prions, a small seabird, which they catch at sea. This is a very dark peregrine with a confiding nature but otherwise just like our British birds back home.

In Britain, peregrines breed on cliffs and hunt over open ground so they occur from the sea coasts of southern England to the highest mountains of Scotland. Most live in the upland areas of Wales, northern England and Scotland but they are also well-distributed along rocky coastlines. In winter, they have a wider distribution and are often found on estuaries and wetlands. About 1,000 pairs of peregrines breed in the United Kingdom, with nearly two-thirds of them occurring in Scotland.

Their fortunes have fluctuated over the years. The loss of forest cover caused by our ancestors would have favoured the open ground hunting peregrines but the advent of firearms and game hunting caused their demise in Victorian times. Then peregrines were killed along with other predators which might interfere with sport. Wartime usually saw an improvement as men went off to fight but in the Second World War peregrines were destroyed in Britain in order to prevent the loss of carrier pigeons bringing back important messages. At least 600 adults were killed during the war and many more eggs and young were destroyed. The bird recovered, however, and it was fully protected in all areas by the Protection of Birds Act of 1954.

In the late 1950s complaints from racing pigeon owners resulted in demands for the bird to be taken off the protected list but this was challenged by the Royal Society for the Protection of Birds. Finally, the government asked the Nature Conservancy to examine this allegation and to determine the distribution and numbers in Britain. Dr. Derek Ratcliffe organised a national survey by the British Trust for Ornithology in 1961 and 1962 when visits were made to all known peregrine haunts in these islands. The results proved that far from being a common bird, half of over 500 traditional nesting sites were no longer occupied and only a quarter of those occupied were producing young. There was clearly something wrong.

I remember taking part in the survey in the central Highlands where numbers had held up better than elsewhere. Eyries were occupied but as my notebooks recall, a nest found with four eggs contained only two a fortnight later and just one at the end of the incubation period which failed to hatch. Like many others it was collected for analysis and allowed Derek Ratcliffe to understand the peregrine's predicament. It was all due to the introduction and widespread use of organo-chlorine pesticides in the 1940s and 50s. These persistent and highly toxic chemicals had entered the food chain and thus the prey species of the peregrine. Being at the top of the food chain, the pesticides had accumulated in the peregrines causing death in old and young birds. It had also caused a reduction in the thickness of the eggshells resulting in breakage, infertility and apparently behavioural problems leading to the birds eating their own eggs. DDT and dieldrin were identified as the main problems and some time later these were banned from use in Britain. Subsequently, numbers recovered and the population is now as high as at any time this century.

Peregrines generally breed at traditional nesting sites on prominent cliffs or crags. Some pairs remain at or near the nesting areas in winter but many of the inland pairs vacate their eyries in the depth of winter, although this is not always the case even in the central Highlands where I have seen single adults at snow and ice covered nesting cliffs. As the days lengthen, activity in the territory increases and by February and early March the pair roost together at the nesting cliff and sometimes hunt together with one bird flushing the prey for the other to catch. The male presents food for his mate as part of their courtship and as spring approaches one or both indulge in spectacular display flights. Sometimes the male will soar high above the nest site and then stoop earthwards with wild abandon in front of the female, or both will play aerial tag. At the cliff, the pair will move from ledge to ledge, chittering to each other and choosing the best nest site. By the time copulation begins they will have scraped out a nest and be ready to start the new season.

Peregrines do not build nests as such, instead they scrape a nest hollow in the earth on a cliff ledge. Some pairs will use the old nests of raven, golden eagle or buzzard. The use of tree nests is very exceptional in Britain but more common elsewhere. In recent years, pairs have nested on artificial ledges on tall buildings and very rarely birds will nest on the ground among heather. Often they nest in exactly the same spot from year to year or even generation to generation. Some pairs may have two or three such chosen places either on the same cliff or on nearby cliffs within the territory. Occupied nests may be from 4 to 10 kilometres apart and occur in Britain from the coast to 800 metres above sea level. Most inland nests occur on moorlands at 300–400 metres' altitude and nesting cliffs may be huge, 300 metres or more, or just tiny crags of 5 metres.

The eggs are laid in late March and April, earlier in the south and later in the higher mountains. The normal clutch is three or four eggs; rarely two or five, the overall average is just over 3.6 per clutch. The eggs are laid at roughly two-day intervals and incubation starts when the penultimate egg is laid. Peregrines lay beautifully marked reddish-brown on buff eggs which vary from bird to bird. Sadly, this means they are highly prized by egg collectors. Some females will re-lay when the first clutch is lost and this takes nearly a month to complete. Incubation is principally by the female with the male covering the eggs for shorter spells during daytime, generally after he has brought food to the nest for the female. The incubating bird sits very tight and often it appears that the nesting cliff is deserted when the male is away hunting and the female is hidden low on the nest ledge. Incubation takes 29 to 32 days per egg and the whole clutch will hatch over a two to three-day period.

During the period of incubation life is quiet at the eyrie, with nothing much to do except sit on the eggs and feed. Of course the weather varies dramatically in Scotland; one day it is bitter with snow showers blasting the cliff face while a few days later the female is panting in the spring heat. This routine is also broken by the neighbours. Often in hilly country a pair of ravens or buzzards may nest nearby, sometimes even on the same cliff. There is usually a sort of amnesty but every now and then someone steps out of line and an aerial fracas breaks out. It is thrilling to watch a male peregrine bombing a raven which at the last moment turns upside down to fend off the attacker. Peregrines also harry eagles and several times I have seen them attack and chase off ospreys. None are actually trying to get at the peregrine's eggs, it is just that they have contravened the airspace regulations, but peace is quickly regained.

When the tiny peregrines come into the world they are covered in white down. They are tended carefully by the female who feeds them with tiny pieces of flesh from prey delivered by the male. Most of the time the female broods the small young to keep them warm including throughout the night; as they mature brooding decreases. Within days they are growing rapidly and call incessantly to be fed. The female delivers the food to each chick without the sibling rivalry displayed by some birds of prey. In fact, as long as peregrine chicks call and beg they will be fed even if they do not belong to that female. Over the years, we have fostered many young peregrines, confiscated by the police from falcon thieves, into nests containing similarly sized young. In all cases, they have been readily accepted including one time when we added three young to a nest of only two chicks. Peregrines may be fantastic at flight but they are no good at arithmetic.

At ten days of age they have grown a second coat of white down, slightly greyer than the first and very woolly in appearance. This is a very busy time for the male who is away hunting from early morning to late evening. On average he should be catching between four and seven birds per day for the growing brood. It is not always easy, even for a peregrine, to catch prey especially in very wet or foggy conditions. Fortunately, as the young grow, the young of other species are fledging and learning to fly and these are easy quarry. In the long daylight hours of the north of Scotland the first feed may be as early as 4am and the last around 11pm, with a distinct tendency to feed the young in the early mornings and evenings, rather than the middle of the day. The male may catch prey up to 4 or 5 miles from the nest and before returning to the eyrie he will have plucked many of the feathers from the carcase. The female, and the brood once they are half-grown, watch for the approach of the male and there is often much excited calling as he returns.

Once at the eyrie, the female takes the prey from her mate and immediately tears up food for the young. The male will usually fly from the eyrie and perch in a favourite place on the surrounding cliffs to rest and preen. The female may take half an hour or more to feed the whole brood after which the young will settle down to digest their food. One summer, I remember observing a peregrine family from a photographic hide overlooking their nest ledge. On one occasion, the male returned with a hooded crow and the female took nearly 40 minutes to feed the carcase to her four young. Even now I can recall those young bloated with food, their crops bulging as they fell asleep in a woolly bundle on the eyrie.

Peregrines hunt and kill a very wide selection of birds; in fact well over 100 different species have been identified in Scotland alone. When feeding young in the inland areas of northern Scotland the most regular prey are domestic pigeons, red grouse, waders such as golden plovers and lapwings, common and black-headed gulls, young crows, rooks and jackdaws and larger songbirds such as mistle thrushes and starlings. On the coast, seabirds such as puffin, kittiwake, fulmar and guillemot are also taken. They often hunt more unusual prey such as tired migrants passing through their territories or birds caught away from their normal haunts. Interestingly, we have found the remains of Manx shearwaters at inland nests in Inverness-shire which were presumably birds trying to fly across land between the Moray Firth and the Minch. Other unusual catches I have seen are great spotted woodpecker, cuckoo, goldeneye, merlin, kestrel and swift. Sometimes the male may have great difficulty in finding food and then quite small prey, such as meadow pipit or wheatear, is brought to the eyrie, but does not satisfy the hunger of the young.

At four weeks of age the young falcons are getting big and starting to moult into the first plumage of feathers. They are very active in the nest and continually preening, watching and wing stretching. This is the time when we visit eyries to ring the young birds and to monitor the progress of different eyries. The eyrie by this stage is littered with the remains of the dead birds eaten by the young, and it is possible to identify the prey from the remains of feathers, legs and beaks on the nest ledge. By five weeks they have moulted most, if not all, of the white down and look very beautiful. Their juvenile plumage has a lovely bloom of colour and they are alert and active. Already there is a clear difference in size between the sexes, especially the size of their legs and feet. They spend much time wing flapping, picking around on the nest and tearing up their own food. Soon they rise a few inches off the nest and at about six weeks they take their first hesitant flights.

Males tend to fly a few days before females and it may be nearly a week before all the young in a brood of four are flying. The first days are spent close to the eyrie, fluttering back and forth in front of the cliff and perching on ledges and convenient trees. Soon they fly out to meet their returning parents, as by now the female is also hunting, and eagerly snatch the prey. Within a few days they have learnt to catch the food in mid-air when released by the parent and to carry it back to the cliff to feed. This is a wonderful time at the nesting cliff as the young gain strength and aerial skills by chasing and playing tag in the sky. All the family roost near the eyrie.

In a week's time, the young are following their parents further away from the nest into the surrounding territory. This is the time they start to learn to hunt. It is a natural step to chase live birds from snatching the dead ones dropped by the parents and it is fortunate for the young peregrines that other young birds are also learning to fly and survive and dopey young pigeons soon come to grief. Within a month, they should all be able to hunt for themselves but in the knowledge that if they fail, there is always a parent to supply food on hungry days. The family stays loosely together and may move to temporary quarters in nearby cliffs but soon autumn approaches and the family finally breaks up.

Young peregrines in Scotland wander farther afield than adults. They tend to move down onto the lower ground and the coastal districts just at the same time as many birds migrate from the northern breeding grounds or from inland to the coast. Some Scottish young have flown to southern Ireland including one youngster which was ringed at its nest at Cape Wrath at the most north-westerly point of Scotland and was later found dead in County Waterford in Eire. Most travellers move shorter distances to southern Scotland and northern Ireland and England. They are not true migrants so some will only move short distances to the nearest estuaries or lower ground. Here they can hunt with relative ease on the plentiful numbers of wintering birds. A big swirl of waders over the mud flats is a pretty sure sign of the presence of a peregrine, and quite often these are birds in their juvenile plumage.

In spring the young peregrines which have survived – the first autumn and winter is the most dangerous time for them – will generally move back to their natal region. Very occasionally they will breed in their first year, more often than not as a result of the death of another bird. Otherwise the young peregrines use the first summer to moult into adult plumage and to investigate potential breeding sites for the following year. Peregrines nesting for the first time are more likely to breed in the region where they were reared but some will nest many miles from home. For example birds reared in northern England have bred in the Highlands. Once they have nested in an area, they are most likely to stay in that territory or nearby. Once established, adults may breed at the same nest for a decade or more, and some can be identified by particular behaviour. I remember one male who used to dive at me so closely that his talons almost combed through my hair as I ringed his young. One year he was gone. Where and how he died I do not know but his place was taken by a new male and the long tradition of peregrines was continued at the cliff. Let us hope that tradition will never be broken for surely that glen would be a poorer place without the cries of peregrines in the spring.

The supreme flier. Peregrine falcons can dive at nearly 200 miles per hour
when in full pursuit of their prey. This one is mobbing an ornithologist
ringing its young in the eyrie. They can also fly long distances
on their powerful wings.

This is a typical nest site in Scotland where most eyries are in cliffs,
especially those with broken, vegetated ledges. The peregrines
scrape out a shallow nest cup on a favourite ledge, often used
for many years, in which the eggs are laid. The ledge also
needs to be large enough to hold the growing family.

Old nests of ravens are sometimes used for nesting by peregrines.

Peregrine falcons normally lay three or four eggs in April. They are beautifully
marked reddish-brown and this is a full clutch. In the pesticide era
of the 1960s, eggs were often thin-shelled and likely to be
broken during incubation. Females sit very tight when
incubating and the eggs hatch after a month.

Peregrine falcons live in many countries of the world. The moors and mountains
around Loch Ness in the Scottish Highlands are a stronghold for them.
In the Falkland Islands, they breed in the coastal cliffs and
hunt far out to sea for small seabirds.

The tiny young are helpless and down-covered when hatched. They are
brooded and fed by the female; at a week they often huddle
together on their own to keep warm. This nest in Finland
is on the ground and the female will need to protect
the chicks from ground predators.

Peregrine Falcon Conservation

For thousands and thousands of years the peregrine falcon has been the supreme predator of the skies, so successful that the species colonised most countries around the world. They have adapted to different habitats from Arctic seacliffs to the African plains as well as to great variations in climate, nest site and prey. The peregrine falcon also has the ability to be either sedentary or a long-distance migrant. Yet industrial man dramatically changed its fortunes in less than a century and we now recognise the peregrine is bound to the biological health of the natural environment.

The most dramatic catastrophe to strike this bird was the secondary effects of the use of agricultural pesticides, such as DDT and dieldrin, in the middle of this century. This caused major declines or extinctions of peregrines throughout the world, but especially in the countries with highly mechanised farming. Fortunately, in our country the bird has shown a remarkable ability to recover since the banning of the most persistent and dangerous pesticides. Nevertheless, it remains true that peregrines are important birds for monitoring on an annual basis because they are such sensitive wildlife indicators. Changes in the quality of their habitat or prey are likely to be discovered from the breeding success and status of the peregrine.

The threat from man-made chemicals still remains and may come from many sources. Organo-chlorine pesticides are still in use in third world countries and some of the birds which form the summer prey of Scottish peregrines winter in Africa, where they may become contaminated. Other prey species winter in coastal areas and estuaries in Britain and Europe where residual levels of contaminants may cause problems when these birds are eaten by peregrines on the breeding grounds. Marine pollutants and their presence in seabirds cause another potential risk for coastal peregrines, and it is of concern that coastal populations in Scotland have not recovered to their former numbers. High levels of poly-chlorinated biphenyls (PCBs) have been found in eggs and dead peregrines. PCBs are industrial chemicals used in the manufacture of plastics, lubricants and insulating materials which have leaked or been dumped into rivers, estuaries and oceans. Dangerous dioxins have been implicated in peregrine breeding failures in coastal California while mercury has been identified in the failed eggs of peregrines in Scotland and elsewhere. The list of chemicals is likely to grow and it is difficult to predict their effects and to apportion blame.

Nevertheless, in much of Scotland the bird is thriving with good populations and healthy breeding success. There are still problems with persecution either by people stealing eggs for illegal collections or by the illegal actions of a minority of people involved in sporting estates. Nests may also be raided for young birds and eggs to supply the falconry trade illegally. This has involved German nationals visiting Scotland but in recent years determined investigative work by the police, customs and the RSPB, assisted by local people, has resulted in successful prosecutions which should help to deter these activities. Even so, vigilance by conservation organisations and the police will be required to maintain the protection this bird deserves.

As the bird recovered in numbers and recolonised its previous range there have been conflicts with people. Some have been specific such as disturbance of a nesting pair by rock climbers. These problems have been well aired in the specialist press and codes of conduct specify that rock climbers move away from nesting cliffs when in use. The more thorny issue arises when peregrines move to a new cliff traditionally used by climbers. In my view it is likely peregrines used such cliffs long before we thought of climbing cliffs and somehow we have to learn to live amicably alongside our neighbours in the natural world. But education and tolerance will be stretched to the limit on those lands where the bird is still destroyed by persons involved in the management and hunting of gamebirds, especially red grouse. On the one hand traditional grouse moors are good for peregrines and on the other they can be dangerous places for the birds to try to breed. Many grouse moor managers accept peregrines as part of the wildlife scene, but others some-how will need to accept that this is a protected bird and not a pest to be killed illegally.

In Scotland, we have two main areas of concern regarding peregrines. One is the seabird cliffs and islands, especially of the north, and the other is the west Highlands and islands. Peregrines have all but disappeared from the Shetland Islands, where I remember them as a striking part of the seabird cliffs at Fair Isle. Now there are none nesting there and their demise is a sad loss. Like elsewhere they would have been subject to pesticides either directly through land birds or through the marine system and seabirds. They also had an unexpected problem. Fulmar petrels, a common seabird around the Scottish coast, spit evil-smelling oil at predators approaching their nests. In the 1960s we found a small number of peregrines in the northern isles dying covered in fulmar oil. Others have been found since. The fulmar population has expanded dramatically this century and many traditional peregrine nesting cliffs are now thronged with fulmars. It is difficult to say whether the fulmar oiling was the principal cause of death or whether the peregrines were already below par from chemical poisoning and thus susceptible to further hazards. Whichever way, it must be an awful death drenched in fulmar oil.

In the west, the problems may also involve marine pollutants but there would also appear to be a food shortage. In many areas of the west Highlands the land has been over-grazed by sheep and deer for several centuries and is often subject to annual large-scale burning. In a landscape of high rainfall, cool climate and acidic rocks this has resulted in decreasing biological quality and a decline in wild prey, especially medium-sized birds such as waders, gamebirds and gulls. This spring as part of the national survey, I visited eight traditional nesting cliffs in Wester Ross and just one was occupied by a breeding pair. Ten years previously six of them were occupied. Of course this is just one year's results and will need further checking. One other change I noted, as well as the birdless over-grazed moors, was the decrease of cultivated land around the crofting townships, which leads to a further decrease in birds such as oystercatchers, lapwings and rock doves.

The very successful programmes of captive breeding and release of peregrines to the wild pioneered in North America demonstrated that endangered birds of prey can be effectively managed. Here in the British Isles, we followed a more conservative approach concentrating on protecting nests especially those colonising new ground. The latter way is effective in some countries but when a local population has become extinct a more hands-on approach has to be tried. It will be interesting to see if peregrines will recolonise Shetland or whether fresh stock will need to be released there to re-establish the bird in those islands. Throughout the world, the peregrine will need to be carefully monitored to ensure its future, and study of the peregrine should surely remind us of the dangers to ourselves of environmental destruction and pollution.

The female feeds the young until they are nearly full-grown.
She takes the prey from the male at the edge of the eyrie
and carries it into the nest where she then finishes
the plucking and starts to feed her brood.

She feeds her youngsters with quite small pieces of prey.

At a month old the young are well feathered.

Their last week in the nest is very hectic for the young peregrines.
They spend much time flapping and strengthening their
wings as well as carefully preening their feathers
ready for flight. The pale tips to feathers are
distinctive of young peregrine falcons.

Estuaries and coastal marshes, like Munlochy Bay on the Moray Firth,
are ideal wintering grounds for peregrines as they are also the
home of large numbers of wildfowl, waders and other
birds in search of the abundant food found
in tidal areas.

In autumn and winter, peregrine falcons can wander great distances
in search of food and suitable wintering places. Their distinctive
silhouette can be seen as they stooge overhead
looking for a potential prey.

The ancient sport of falconry – man, dog and bird.

This peregrine falcon flown by a falconer has killed a red grouse
on a heather moor in Scotland and is guarding
its prey by mantling its wings and
tail over the dead bird.

In open farmland, grey partridges are a favourite prey and a
good meal able to sustain a peregrine falcon
for several days.

Enjoying Peregrine Falcons

'There's a peregrine!' 'Where?' 'There, over the trees. Oh, sorry, it's dived round the hill.' Many, many times have I had similar conversations when I have suddenly seen a fast flying peregrine and my companions have failed to see it through their binoculars before it dived out of view. They can be seen just about anywhere and usually there is not much time to watch them. Away from the nesting areas, they tend to stooge across the sky with a surprisingly proprietorial manner, suddenly bursting into speed to catch prey or sometimes it seems just to test the flying skills of flocks of birds. Otherwise, they roost in cliffs or prominent trees, or man-made structures such as pylons and bridges. There they while away the hours just quietly watching the world go by.

The presence of a peregrine is more often than not given away by the panic among the rest of the bird population. On estuaries huge flocks of waders will suddenly rise from the mud and swirl around in formation, tightly packed and letting the hunter know he has been seen. To find the peregrine you need to scan the horizon or, if the hunt is on, to look for the most panic-stricken group. More often than not you see the bird after the hunt, either lugging the prey back to a favourite feeding perch or being hounded out of the area by the bravest birds.

Nowadays, people often see them at nest sites, some of which can be surprisingly close to public places, with even a few on buildings within towns. The most important thing to remember is to put the welfare of the bird first. If the peregrines are calling with their strident 'kek-kek-kek' call then you are too close to the nesting site and should leave. Remember, the peregrine is specially protected under the Wildlife and Countryside Act and it is an offence to intentionally disturb it when at its nest.

Some eyries are now well-known and can be viewed without any disturbance. One of the best known is at Symond's Yat Rock in Gloucestershire where the Forestry Commission and the Royal Society for the Protection of Birds have provided a public viewing place overlooking a peregrine nesting cliff since 1984. The site is in a spectacular cliff overlooking the river Wye. The observation post is manned by the RSPB from April to August and there are powerful telescopes trained on the birds. An educational programme about peregrines is also provided.

Peregrine Falcon Facts

Other Names:

Gaelic – Seabhag   **Swedish** – Pilgrimsfalk
German – Wanderfalke   **Russian** – CahПah
French – Faucon pèlerin   **Dutch** – Slechtvalk
Spanish – Halcón común   **Danish** – Vandrefalk
Italian – Falco pellegrino

Scientific name: *Falco peregrinus*

Races or sub-species:

22–24 races worldwide including:
F.p.peregrinus: Britain and northern Europe
F.p.brookei: southern Europe
F.p. calidus: arctic Europe
F.p.pelegrinoides: north Africa
F.p.anatum: north America

Breeding population:

Scotland	approx 600 pairs
United Kingdom	approx 1,000 pairs
Europe	approx 6,000 pairs

Measurements (average for *peregrinus*):

	male	female
Length (cms)	40–45	45–49
Wingspan (cms)	79–89	93–100
Tail (cms)	13–16	16–19
Weight (gms)	700	1,100

Breeding:
Age at first breeding usually 2 years
Single-brooded

Clutch size: 3–4, occasionally 2, rarely 5
Egg size: (mms) 51.5 × 40.8

Fresh weight of egg: 45 gms
Incubation period: 28–33 days
Fledging period: 40–42 days

Plumage characteristics:
First down plumage at hatching
Second down from 10 days
First complete feathers 35 days
Full adult plumage 16 months

Recommended Reading

The Peregrine Falcon by Derek Ratcliffe, published by Poyser, 1980 is the acknowledged monograph on the species. This most important and detailed book has been updated by the author and its re-publication is imminent. The bibliography outlines the very extensive literature on the peregrine, including many scientific papers worldwide.

Biographical Note

Roy Dennis is a professional ornithologist living near Loch Garten in the Scottish Highlands. For 8 years in the 1960s, he and his wife ran the Bird Observatory on Fair Isle, famous for bird migration and seabirds. From 1971 to 1991, he was the RSPB's senior officer in the Highlands and is now a self-employed wildlife consultant. He is a specialist on birds of prey and has been involved in all four national peregrine surveys since 1961. He is a well-known lecturer, broadcaster and writer.